Poems from Whimsy Manor

Jeanette Purkis © 2018

Published by Healthy Possibilities, Adelaide, South Australia.

Contents

Introduction 3
Storming the Winter Palace and other Sunday activities 4
    Manifesto 4
    Untitled 5
    The fringe 7
    Monday 8
    Small talk 10
    An overachiever's reflection 11
    The Guardian 12
    Reconciliation 13
    I don't want your cure 16
    Auspicious Day 17
    Shadow girl 19
A Naughty Autie at the Age of Forty (and some months…) 23
    Supermarket ructions 25
    An assuredly adult adult 26
    The ordinary club 27
    My work is a perfect thing 28
    Mum 30
    I give talks 32
    My children 34
    Too kind 35
    Reunion 36
    They don't grieve, do they? 37
    Messages in the twilight 38
    My world 39
    Not quite enough 41
    The wisdom of youth 43

- Being me 45

When the brain is a pain: little bit creative, little bit crazy 47
- Untitled.   [CW - alludes to sexual violence] 48
- Diagnosis - reflections on application of 'schizophrenic' to my me 50
- Lament of the deranged deity 51
- My private universe 53
- Lost 55
- Altered 57

Life: filling your hours full of minutes and cuddling your kitty 60
- When I get old 61
- On my feline friends and confidantes 62
- The Rearguard Vanguard 63
- And Melbourne sparkles 65
- Little panther 66
- The nation of me 67
- Goodbye good readers. 68

Introduction

Welcome readers. This is a little book of poetry I have put together for your enjoyment and consideration.

I am a little author person who lives in an apartment with a good supply of art and a big, purry black cat who goes by the name of Hieronymus Bosch Kitty Purkis II, or Mr Kitty to his friends.

I started writing poetry when I was eight years old and never really stopped. The poems in this book were all written some time between 2011 and 2018. I am the resident author at Whimsy Manor. I love to work and work and work some more! I also work in a professional job, then I come home and write books and presentations and talk to about 10,000 people on social media (but not all at once!) I am a proud member of the Autistic Neurodivergent Quirky Purky tribe and also a paid up member of the Mental Health Connoisseurs Club.

Poetry is a luxury. A little treat like a chocolate at the end of dinner. The poetry here ranges from the fun and observational to the challenging, reflective and melancholy.

Any writing which is potentially triggering has a content warning next to the title (which looks like this: 'CW'), as, while challenging perceptions is a good thing, upsetting people with dark things they are not in the space for is not.

There are some artworks and other images throughout the text. Art and poetry go so well together. Art and mathematics do too I think but it is not as widely acknowledged.

So, come with Mr Kitty and I on a trip through what John Keats - a far superior and considerably more dead poet than me - termed 'visions of poesy.' Welcome to Whimsy Manor. Sign the guest book on your way in, play with one of many things that has 'fidget' in its name, and laugh at Mr Kitty being playful and silly and climbing inside your handbag. Tell me how you like your cup of tea and whether we should get pizza or Thai food.

Jeanette

Storming the Winter Palace and other Sunday activities

Manifesto

I am not beige, taupe or pastel tones.

I am not timid and unassuming.

I will not stand idly by if I need to speak up.

I am for rainbows and glitter.

I am loud.

I laugh so hard I snort and then laugh some more.

I am for love and fierce passion.

I am big and bright.

I am for a revolution in the art gallery.

I am for typewriters and poetry dripping its literary juices and changing everything.

I am for the unlikely, the strange, the impossible and the quirky.

I am for cats - all of them.

I am for life.

I am for difference and diversity.

I am for music all the day long and dancing alone in the kitchen.

Untitled

She unlocks the door

The shelves with their shiny glass statues and certificates

An accomplished someone lives here

She reminds herself - 'It is me'

Odd that

Accomplished is not her sense of her

Broken down, tired

An impostor

She turns on the machine

Clinging to her online family

Yet the connection is not always connected

An often empty world

Charlatans to avoid

Perhaps there is nothing there in the land beyond her monitor and mouse

She doesn't know praise from criticism

Maybe this isn't real?

Each evening passes

Repeats of Spicks and Specks and Little Britain and Friends

Some writing - she remembers her author-hood

Finds herself in the 'zone', or some zone - hard to tell which one. The different zones are so similar in appearance

A chapter flows forth from the digital wellspring

Meaning comes in nouns and verbs

The inner world meets the real world

Its conduit gently shuts down the computer and goes to bed.

Another day gone, another yet to come

The fringe

I am woman on the fringe, at the quirk

I'm Frida's sister

I'm Nico's child

I'm the one you warned your daughters about

I laugh loud, holding my belly then clapping my hands

I am not polite or shy

I take the last biscuit enthusiastically, with ownership and investment

I don't want a good man

I'm not settling down

I don't want fashion and fascinators and painful towering heels

I am your mum wearing army boots

I will not be a domestic goddess, whatever that is

I refuse compromise

I will be me, whatever it takes

I'll 'corrupt' young girls with ideas of art and poetry

When I die people will not mourn timidly in a damp church on uncomfortable pews

They will dance around my grave wearing purple and green

Drinking wine deeply

Celebrating birth and death and the mayhem in between

Yes, I am a proudly a woman

A woman of full life and quirky manner

I am my self at every moment

It is a good life

Monday

(CW - psychiatric hospital)

Monday

I put on my suit - armour against the sword of daily life

I took the bus to work

Thoughts passed through my mind

of awful and inappropriate actions.

I swiped my card. The perspex doors gave way at its bidding and I was in the lift I got out at Level 5, walked to my desk and logged on

The emails made no sense

I took myself to a private room and called Kathy, my capable clinical manager "Go home" she said

but I was determined.

After what seemed no time my manager was driving me to see Kathy, concerned. The world seemed to close in - there was no future

Kathy was concerned as well - worry etched in her features.

A trip to the hospital

Waiting

I escaped. Kathy gave chase.

Police walked by

I looked longingly at their guns

but what sort of public servant would that make me I thought?
A dead one.

Kathy leaves me at the assessment unit

In my suit.

My make-up perfect, jewellery matching my clothes

Work shoes newly polished.

There is no tomorrow I think, at least, not one in which I want to be.

The psychiatrist - young, cocky, male - sends me to PSU, the locked ward, for my own protection.

I arrive that night

In my suit.

"Do you work here?" asks an intern

"no" I respond gloomily. "I'm just a well-dressed patient."

Outside the rebels storm the winter palace and the sky explodes
Inside I'm safe, medicated and confused.

The world goes on around me, unaware and unconcerned

Small talk

Making the morning brew
Colleagues crowding in the kitchen "How was your weekend?"

My weekend:

Friday evening reprieve

No more internal conversations while trying to pay attention to the real people and not the ghosts

No more corridor paranoia of whispered insults from impossible places

I'm up until 3 am

hunched over the laptop like some latter day Quasimodo

No bells here for Esmerelda save for Facebook notifications and message alerts

Sleepy Saturday spent assessing the state of my sanity

"Do I need to call the Crisis Team?'

"Don't waste their time idiot girl. They don't want to talk to you.' 'I'm a public servant. I'm an author. I should be OK. I should ....'
Then the scary question

'do I need to go to hospital??'

No not an option. Those conferences won't keynote themselves
After cryptic social media conversations a friend invites herself to my house. 'It's a mess' I start but she doesn't care.

We spend Sunday watching DVDs. She brought coconut water.

Evening when my friend and liberator leaves.

Monday comes.

Put on the suit, the makeup and the cloak of Confidence.

Go to work.

We made it!

I'm straight into the kitchen for the morning brew.

"How was your weekend?' A forced smile - I'm the expert

I can make my eyes smile even when my world is dying

"Good" I say."how about you?"

An overachiever's reflection

I'm in my hotel room, lying in the extra comfy bed listening to music.

I think 'What do I need to do now?'

'Nothing' is the realisation.

I think about this for a while. 'Really, nothing??' I ask myself incredulously.

Yep, nothing at all. You can watch Netflix, read a book, just lie here and enjoy not doing things with an output attached.'

I'll have to think about this a bit more….

In the meantime room service is on its way and there is a craft beer in the minibar which may need sampling

Leisure seems to be a surprisingly satisfying pursuit

Seriously though,

I have Nothing To Do??

Wow

The Guardian

I like the sun

Lie in the warm spots even in summer

I like to play

Running around the house, jumping on things

Just a little destructive with all the exuberance

I like to eat

In distant history there was no food

I eat quickly now, in case the food supply dries up

I like to cuddle

My person holds me close and talks softly

I don't understand the words but I like to listen
I am her guardian

I don't go out - I don't need to

There is ample entertainment here - birds outside the window, the neighbourhood cat who torments me.
I yell at him under the front door in meow

When my person is sad I talk to her in purrs
She rescued me, so I can rescue her

Her sadness is a presence in the house

I try to banish it and save my saviour
I sit next to her as she works
At the end of the day I snuggle next to her in the big bed. Kitty heaven!

My person puts her arm around me and holds my paw We go to sleep like this, ready for another day

Mr Kitty at Curtin Cat Care 2017

Reconciliation

I'm tired

Seventeen years of tired

Of metaphorically jerking my neck around to spy my past then run from her as fast as I can.

Excuses excuses

'I'm not like that...

'She isn't me. She is previous me...'

He face leers grotesquely in the mirror

Every time success comes my way she is right next to me, taunting, blaming, hating.

Hard to express just how I hate her
Every act is framed by her presence. I can't really own my life

Every day at my job

Accepting accolades and planning what to do if she ever escapes to destroy all I have made

I had no future than and I barely see one now

"If good things happen I will be dead straight afterwards'

'Don't get too comfortable. You were in prison. Everyone will know and they will hate you

There is no good in you. You are just pretending.

Others can see past your nice act to who you really are. You are ME.

Oh I shall destroy you. All those who love you will hate you when I'm done. Author? positive person? Autism world Celebrity? Really? Who do you think you are?

I step back and watch the person I once was

I see her desperation

I see that every kind word I say, each decent act I commit puts a distance between us.

She is desperate

As she always was

She is both victim and perpetrator.

Vulnerable

Young

Scared

Acting tough in a world really not fit for her

The hatred is an act. Mostly

She learned the words, the attitude, but was never really there.

I summon up my strength and approach her.

She's like a frightened dog - hackles up and in need of love and closeness. Tentatively I hold my hand to her

"You can be yourself' I say

'There is eighteen years between you and I. This world will accept you

Forgive your mistakes and support you.

You don't need to fight the world.

There is a place for you.

There is a cat....'

I edge closer

I touch my hand to her. It is scarred but she holds on tight

We embrace

gingerly at first, both of us wondering what the other may do

Then she grabs me and holds me close

She cries and I wipe her tears as she does for me

My shadow self and I together

I hold no fear of her

It is swept away amid understanding and acceptance.

Untitled, Jeanette Purkis 2017

I don't want your cure

I don't want your cure

I am not broken

I don't belong condemned to the genetic dustbin
I am not less

My world is not 'wrong'

My communication not 'lacking'

My interests not 'obsessive'.

I am not a tragedy

Not the product of a cruel God

Not something to be fixed.

I am myself

I am proud and beautiful

My reality as valid as your reality

My experience my own.

I love my world

This world I share with others like me
The only tragedy in my life is hatred
People too small to see my value

Too sad to delight in my quirks
You want a cure

Which part of me will you cure?

Will you cure my talent?

The brilliance of my pen

The clarity of my wit?

Will you take my life and remove all the broken bits?

All the life I have lived

The wisdom gained through horror and loss?

The love and kindness left when the fires of abuse and terror died?
Will you take my compassion

My empathy

My love for the Other?

What of me would you leave behind from your cure?

No. I don't want your cure.

I want your understanding, your ear, free of judgement.
I am human

There is no cure for humanity save death

And that is hardly a cure.

Auspicious Day

Mr Kitty turned three today

Part of his charm and quirk to be born on April fools day.

He was on my bed in the morning, snuggly by my feet

He gave his customary morning smooch then bit me for good measure.

We played together with a wand and catnip mouse (the things they dream of these days!)

Autism day today apparently. (Why is it just one day?)

My services were called upon to launch things. Probably unpopular if i launch into an argument I suppose

My day proper began at the Southern Cross Club

A palace of poker machines and meat raffles. Their restaurant menu straight out of 1973.

Suited, booted and made-up I bypassed the poker machines for the rarified atmosphere of the private dining room (it had paintings).

My talk is set for 10 am.

I walk to the lectern, clutching the crumpled page which is my presentation

I have the audience. They are mine for this brief moment.

The interchangeable neurotypical notables always love the lived experience person

The success story and actor which is me on the stage.

I get a loud applause.

The politician following me mentions my talk

A lot.

I think I upstaged her.

Is that something neurotypical keynotes know not to do? It wasn't intentional. Now I'm worried.

I wonder how you apologise for this crime?

I forget the worry as I am swamped by apparently every CEO and board member in the Autism world

(I secretly do the thing where I try to diagnose one or other of them).

Someone asks me to speak at her conference with Temple Grandin

Temple, the ultimate role model

And me, the Autism world's Clark Kent - bureaucrat one moment, 'hero' the next. Of course this large unwieldy piece of knowledge doesn't sink in

Until 100 people profess to 'like' it on social media.

I get home unsure of what just happened.

The birthday cat awaits me with meows and purrs

He sits on my lap as I scroll through messages and random thoughts.

He bites me, admonishing my distraction from attending to his affections.
I turn my attention to this furry boy

I hold him close and bury my face in his black softness.

I reflect on a saying of mine, immortalised in meme 'There is nothing like the bond between an Aspie and her cat'.

And it is true.
This little creature, filled with purrs and bites and naughty,

With midnight storms through the house, up and down the bed, behind the couch
With love bubbling from him

With his patented Mr Kitty 'Mraow'

This little being who I care for more than anything

Three years ago was born.

And I know more than I know my own name that in this cat is more value than any successes, books media appearances, renown and glory.

He is more than everything.

This cat makes me something more human. He is my gift

I am grateful. Yes indeed. An auspicious day.

Shadow girl

There was once a girl with a happy laugh and a curious smile.
But she did not know it.

For she lived in the shadows

Where the creatures of the dark hurt her

They told her lies and called her names. She hated the shadow world

But it was her home.

She wanted to leave her broken world

but she couldn't find her way into the fresh green garden she believed was above
She imagined its flowers and birds and dragonflies humming by happily.

The shadows broke her spirit and took the smile from her eyes
The love from her heart

The will from her mind.

Weighed down, she trolled the shadows, crying silently. For she knew this was not her home

But she couldn't come out.

One day she started to walk

went to places she hadn't been

Ghosts laughed at her and made bets that she would be here forever but she just kept on walking.

One day she found a rock stair case

She looked up and saw stars - actual, beautiful twinkling stars

Lights calling to her straight from the very beginning of the universe.

Even though the stairs were slimy and she feared she would fall with every step she knew she needed to go

It was her only chance to be free.

She went on and on.

Hours and days and years elapsed

Strangely, the higher she got - even though the danger of falling grew worse with each footfall - she started to feel renewed and confident.

Clear crisp air filled her lungs.

She started to smell blossoms - so far from the foul odours of the shadows, smells of death and decay and defeat.

As she climbed higher, beams of light started to shine on her face. The light was warm and gave her hope.

She saw the top of the stairs

She took a tentative step into this new world. She looked down and saw her dress was white

Her hair like spun gold flowing down past her shoulders.

She lay in the green grass in the garden looking up at a pure blue sky. She couldn't find a word for what she felt

She didn't even know what she felt except that she was no longer afraid.

An age passed.

The garden was so beautiful but the girl was all alone

What point is there to happiness if one can't share the experience? The girl thought.

As soon as she thought that, a little black cat strode over, exuding cat confidence He wound himself around her legs.

She stroked the cat and felt his soft fur.

The cat walked off into the distance

"Wait!' the girl said and followed him, running to keep up.

She followed the cat for a long while,

Damp, springy grass underfoot.

He stopped at the top of the staircase.

She looked down and saw shadows and ghosts. They looked weighed down and sad.

She wondered how she could help.

The cat started walking down the stairs.

The girl followed.

It seemed infinitely easier going down than it had been coming up.

The girl met a ghost

But the ghost was not frightening or evil - it was sad.

Against all logic, the girl held out her hand to the ghost

With the touch she saw the ghost's humanity

It was a young girl with spiky red hair, green eyes and a tentative smile. The ghost was a friend.

The two of them went hand in hand up the stairs, followed by the cat.

It was infinitely more easy to traverse the stairs with company,

The two girls talked and laughed and helped each other up.

The cat showed them the best way to ascend and purred a tune to keep them inspired.

As they ascended, the ghosts took on stronger form
After while the two of them looked like sisters.
They were whole.

So the girl spent eternity rescuing ghosts from the fetid world below. She took them to the garden where they could live their new existence. She became friends with each one of them.

The task would never be done but the rewards were great.

And the garden became filled with the laughter of children and adults who once were shadows but were now whole, fulfilled, free people.

And the girl kept on at her task.

A Naughty Autie at the Age of Forty (and some months...)

The poems in this chapter relate to All Things Autism, which in my case means pretty much everything in my life. I was diagnosed with Aspergers at twenty, way back in 1994 when most people thought 'Asperger's' was a green vegetable often used in mildly amusing sexual innuendo gags and which goes well with a poached egg and parmesan cheese). I didn't care for the asparagus -related humour or accept the diagnosis. When I did - seven years later - I was almost ashamed of my diagnostic 'label' and it wasn't so much that I disclosed as I admitted it, like a shameful secret. Only then to people I knew I could trust not to chase me out of town waving torches and pitchforks. Thankfully I got over that when my autobiography, Finding a Different Kind of Normal [insert shameless authorial book plug here] came out in 2006. Even then most of the questions I got asked at presentations left me inwardly baffled and outwardly winging it. Things are a little different now and I am an out loud and proud Autistic woman who loves talking about my life and work with anyone, including the occasional taxi driver and all of ,y work colleagues.. Autism is me, my identity, my world. She is inseparable from my character and integral to my very being.

Jeanette in a purple pixie hat and Mr Kitty in a black fur onesie, 2017

Supermarket ructions

Oh supermarket, you are really not my friend.

Why do you have to continually disappoint me?
I need you in my life, but not like this.

Is there a law that states you need obnoxious and oblivious old folk to block the aisles?

To ask me to find some mystery food item that I've never heard of amongst all the horrible choice?

To push in front of me in queues, apparently desperate to cram their remaining days with bargains and special offers?

Why do you insist on stocking bleach? The noxious smell spreads its tendrils into whole sections of your space. (And I seem to be the only one aware of its putrid toxicity)

Why are your staff so oblivious to my plight?

When I stand in line my anxiety takes on a life of its own

I hasten to stack my items on the conveyer before one of your minions packs the bread under the cat food

Then comes the barrage of questions

'Cash or card?'

'Do you want to buy a bag?'

'Do you have an everyday rewards card?' (what is an everyday rewards card??)
'Jamie Oliver recipe cards ma'am?'

Confused and cranky, I rush out of there as soon as I can.

So supermarket, why won't you be my friend?

Why can't you give a little? Concede some ground?

Why do you have to be so mean?

I want to get along but you seem determined to stymie my attempts at friendship.

If you don't lift your game I might have to shop online.
I don't think you would really miss me.

An assuredly adult adult

I'm forty-three

I work full-time

Then spend just as long in my job as official and largely unpaid autism advocate
I might not drive

but I did go overseas by myself for a month

And gave a lecture tour - they paid me

I own my home

And I moved out of 'home' as was at the surprising age of seventeen

I have a Masters degree

Student loans

And an understanding of art theory and French philosophy that would baffle the most studious of scholars.

I'm sad to say that I have a dark, nasty, evil past
But even criminal Jeanette was tried as an adult
I was an adult.

I am an adult
I have been for so very many years. Then why

Seriously, Why

Am I a little child in your eyes?
As are my Autistic sisters and brothers.
What do you see when you look at us?
Why, when we are so capable
Sensitive

Accomplished

Masterful

Do you still see a little child?
I will say one thing: we are not children

It may be one thing but I apparently must say it over again

always, forever and ever Amen.
See me as I am

Please grant me that one measly right
And know that I am forty-three, not four

The ordinary club

Ordinary people are vague

I have executive functioning issues

Ordinary people 'wake up on the wrong side of the bed'
I have difficulty regulating my emotions

Ordinary people 'don't get it'
I have no theory of mind

Ordinary people love their car

I have an unusual fascination with inanimate objects

Ordinary people have a party trick
I am an 'idiot savant'

Ordinary people live their lives doing the best they can. They go to work, study, raise kids, go on holidays and nobody much notices.

When I do any of these I am 'an inspiration'

Apparently I don't belong in the ordinary people club No, it's true.

I belong in the extraordinary people club

Which is altogether more satisfying.

My work is a perfect thing

Each morning of each weekday

I board a bus into civic

And go to work.

I am one of nature's civil servants - I have been for eleven years,
But maybe forever (at least since my brother and i played offices as kids)

Me, that little enthusiastic Autie sprite

Who bounces from my desk

to the printer

And smiles so broadly

For what my colleagues might not know is that in fact career Jeanette died some years ago

And is now ensconced in that open plan office which is work heaven.

For years I struggled

At fast food counter

and charity collector's purgatory and blight.

For a while I was a kitchenhand
Hell's kitchenhand to be precise
Hunched over the boiling sink with dermatitis hands

And impending psychosis from the stress and steam.

And then years later I find my world turned upside down
Not the socialist utopia - for that dream is long forgotten
But in blissful bureaucratic paradise of Ministerials and sticky flags

Perfect order

A seemingly seamless hierarchy filing and folders

briefings

all manner of stationery.

How - but how - did I find my way to this place?

Others may query and quibble on wages and conditions, but here is me, looking out at the view from the tenth floor
A view that goes to forever.

And yes, my work is a heaven of its kind

I scarcely believe my luck to be here

Even after eleven years.

And my Autistic self is attuned to this life,

Respected and included.

My troubles banished through distraction and focus on the task at hand
My intellect harnessed

My experiences valued by managers and colleagues

I might inadvertently irritate some

or wear my welcome thin with my quirky extrovert joy

But this is my home.

I still proudly say 'I work in the department.

I am a public servant'

For this has been my destiny since my graduate year. I'm unsure whether I will remain
or leave for 'greener pastures'
or maybe just use my greenest pen.

Yes my work is a perfect thing.

I thank whichever employment gods put the thought in my mind as I looked at CareerOne all those years before

the thought: 'Public service? Yeah, I could do that.'
And yes, I could.

Note: The original version of this poem formed part of a birthday gift for a wonderful manager who became good friends with Jeanette, complete with images

Mum

My mum is not the average mum

She never gossiped with her girlfriends at the school gate

She never wore heels

or make-up.

She did have three lipsticks from the 1970s - a pink one and orange one and and sort of melted brown blob

She didn't ever watch rom-coms

She stopped buying music in about 1963.

She never talked about being a lady

or using your feminine wiles

(whatever those were).

She tromped around the garden in gumboots

and a jumper from the dark ages.

When I was little there were lots of books

Little kid books

Christian books

then books we could read by ourselves.

One day my mum read a magical book from her childhood. It was precious, A treasure.

She only read it to us once to keep the pages from falling out.

It was from the ancient history that was my mum's own difficult childhood
She read it as if preserving her fragile history

Stopping its few good memories from disintegrating into crumbs.

Mostly my mum's idea of calming reading was the book of Revelation.

At 10 I knew all about the Whore of Babylon

But I'd never watched Mary Poppins.

My mum had a word for every occasion

a logophile

(ironic that one needs to be a logophile to know what one is).

In a sea of Englishness she sported an Australian twang.

England was always too cold.

too windy

she'd set up a vivid orange tent on every English beach

We never got lost

We'd see the tent's toxic hue and come whirring back like homing pigeons If pigeons like dribbly ice cream and seaside rock.

As I got older my mum transformed
She was now my best friend

In the absence of friends my age. I could tell her anything

I'd stand behind her and brush her hair, hundreds of times

Thousands when measured in days and months and years.
Whenever I was in trouble she'd be there

Ready

Amazing.

Some time after I gained for myself a label

'Jeanette:Autist'

I went through adulthood the lone labelled person in our quirky Purky world.

It was almost a sleight - why just me when others in our midst may benefit from a swipe from the label machine?

One Christmas I was home

My mum comes up with unknown intent

She thrusts a card into my hand

'I want the assessment. Give me the label' it read

Clinician visited

Label attached.

My mum, my friend, my champion all along is now in the club -

we are in it together:
The same

Our perfect club of two within the larger club we've been in all these years.
Our labels bear the same name

'Thank you mum'

I give talks

I give talks

Talks about Autism mostly I write them for schools Conferences, workplaces - anything really.

I've launched events
Been a keynote

An expert

An invited speaker I've put in abstracts Submissions

Pleas and supplications.

I've been singled out from the podium

('It's an honour to have Jeanette in the audience')

I've been ignored

Called the wrong name

My bio read off a scrap of paper - complete with typo.

I wonder sometimes if I have groupies

I know there are tall poppied people who hate me

You tend to lose your humanity once you are 'the competition'.

But I am still not oblivious to their rudeness

If I am to be a robot I must be Marvin - paranoia intact and sensitivity charged. I get questions from parents

Stressful those - for I cannot always fix the issue, no matter how desperate the plea

Challenging, engaging comments from fellow advocates

Even an occasional argument from a variety of quarters.

When I give talks I become an oddity

An object of uncomfortable respect.

As if this activity I do for pleasure is of some rare value.

But my non-work work is just a function, like baking a cake, hugging a child, cleaning the streets.

Though I do love my vocation

Each time I climb those steps

A moment before I launch into my recitative

My refrain

I stop for a moment

Smile at the people in their hard seats

Utter to myself the same mantra

'Let's do this thing. Let's change the world.'

And I hope in my little, unimportant, incidental way, that I will.

My children

'You need children in your life'

So says an interchangeable elderly relative

I am evidently deficient in children
Perhaps in womanhood.

A strange, proprietary thought.
I need my own offspring to be fulfilled as a woman a human. I could yell 'Ableist! Sexist!'

Yet I'm less offended,
more disappointed at the insightless ignorance.
For it is untrue.

I have children in my life
My entire purpose is for them
Surely I must be a parent of some sort?

I don't know each child by name but they are there
Driving my choices
shining into my knowledge with their unseen presence.

This physical distance from those I value is my choice
A me-child would cripple me with anxiety

They would never leave my house from my fear of accident or incident.

My imagined offspring are relieved that they have not seen light of day. I am better suited to the children I have

Autistic kids, their siblings, their parents.

Sullen teens with their latent potential

exuberant, creative girls dancing barefoot in the garden
Their parents - bursting with love and concern

Seeking solutions with open ears.

These may not be my flesh and blood children but my children by proxy
Yet I delight in their being and love them as a additional aunty

That is enough to fulfil this human.

Too kind

'You're too kind'

As I'm told everyday.

'Why don't you ask for money?

You really should get paid for all of this that you do'

'You should tell people 'no, I can't help.'

'Those people are sucking the life out of you Jeanette'.

(And so often if I vent to a neurotypical type, the same response: 'Oh, are they on the spectrum?')

I'm not too kind, I don't want money

If I can help I won't say 'no'

And my lifeblood being sucked by people in pain and trouble? It's a risk I'm prepared to take.

And as to the last, oh yes, that last little thing

I count amongst my social media comrades a multitude

Most are Autistic, like me.

Ad of all those people, I have need to vent following their exchanges and queries perhaps twice a year.

And if I have need to turn on the assertiveness switch

To ask them to do whatever they're doing in some different way

each time they apologise and stop doing their irritant thing.

No grudges

No judgement

No snidey comments behind my back.

Maybe when someone vents to me I should pose the question

'Oh, but are they neurotypical?'

Reunion

It's an awards night

National recognition for Autistic legends or some such thing But really it's a reunion

Of friends

And rivals

And perhaps the odd enemy.

Everyone's putting it on social media

'I'm nominated!'

'I might win!'.

Strange that we're so competitive when we get together
Always the same

But I'm like it too.

I want to win

I'll be the best

Why does it matter who got to speak at what and who's book is a bestseller? Why do I care?

I'm happy

employed

alive

Surely that's enough.

I challenge the fame monster

'You will not have me'

'I am not your conduit, your slave.'

She grows weaker

I care less.

My mum sits in my mind with the book of Proverbs

'Pride cometh before a fall and a haughty spirit before destruction'
Maybe God and my mum have a point - they are a formidable partnership.

So I step back

Focus on what I have

It's like letting go.

Awards night is friends night now Not a competition.

They don't grieve, do they?

I was told by the doctor that I don't grieve. 'Autistics don't grieve.' she pronounced 'You don't feel love

or empathy.'

So why then did I feel like my world was ruined and gone

That part of my soul was missing when cancer took Val to a place I couldn't follow If it wasn't grief?

What was the rush of joy which filled me full of closeness and wonder when I held my brand new niece in my arms

if it wasn't love?

Why then have I spent years doing endless unpaid work to assist others if I am devoid of empathy?

Maybe the doctor showed me that she lived in a world devoid of love and empathy.

Maybe I should help show her my love

my empathy

My grief
To make her whole?

Messages in the twilight

She sends me a message

'Please look at my blog'

I promise to oblige, silently grumbling and moaning 'People wanting my time

Never leave me alone

Crappy public profile.....'

Next day I read the blog
Scanning for ableism
Paternalism

Negativity

And heaven forbid, the hated anti-vax sentiments, but there is none.

('Messages in the Twilight' continued)

There is more

of beauty

the sentiments of care

I almost cry

(I never cry)

So poignant

So perfect

Images

Words

Experiences laid out for me with a pink background on my screen

This mother and her care

Her children leap from the screen

I want to hug them

but don't know whether such familiarity is appropriate
Acceptable

I've glimpsed into a rare beauty

Sad and perfect

This woman - on the periphery of my apparently endless social network
She is now my friend

I hold her close through the ten thousand miles

The deep fathoms of ocean which separate us physically

We are close

One

'I will not let you go

Let me hold your fragile thought, the unbearable concern that is your words

Will you hold my words too?'

We are wrapped in a virtual embrace

I imagine us here forever

Sad but perfect.

I treasure the message that brought me into your world. Thank you

My world

My world is filled with stars

and beauty of red sparkles and silver shiny things.

My world is filled with love
Of cats

And art

And certain people.

My world is filled with work
With presentations

and spreadsheets

and goals.

My world is filled with music
With singing

and dancing

and stimming.

My world is filled with memory
With sadness

And abuse

And regret.

My world is filled with experience

With autism

and achievement

and heroes.

My world is filled with wonder
With science

and mystery

and intellect.

My world is filled with me. I am different, not less

I am my own being, valued as all others.

Drawing, December 2017, J Purkis

Not quite enough

'You're not Autistic enough to say you're Autistic'

'You don't look Autistic'

'Jeanette only has very mild Asperger's. She has no right to say she's Autistic' '
My nephew/son/sister/insert random relative/ is ACTUALLY Autistic, not like you.'

'You could pass for normal'.

I respond almost defensively

As if i need to defend my right to share something I was diagnosed with y a specialist.

As if the topic people pay me to speak about - from personal experience, the topic of the several books I have penned

The community I so delightedly and gratefully belong to

Is not where I fit.

Few things spur me to anger

I am patient and kind

I try hard not to judge

But this 'not quite Autistic enough'
Not quite stereotypical enough

Not quite male enough

Not quite enough of your expectations
Not quite broken enough…

You're not quite enough is just enough to make me leave my patience behind Drop my kindness and launch into invective and fury.

If I'm not quite Autistic enough

Maybe you are not quite considerate enough

Not quite evolved enough

Not quite decent enough
Not quite empathetic enough

Not quite respectful enough

Not quite tactful enough

Not quite human enough?

To be counted among the list of people I value.

The wisdom of youth

He's sitting next to me

blond hair

beautiful - if pimple-pocked - face
Exuberant

Smiley

We laugh at the same bits of the talk

Wave at the speaker\

His dad next to him, looks concerned

Just the faintest glint of judgement in his manner At this big lady

Laughing like a child

With his child

This forty-something Autist

with public service lanyard dangling incongruously from her neck.

After the talk we keep laughing together

kindred spirits across the chasm of years and varied experience

He is Thomas

I am Jeanette.

The speaker is Graeme

And his book is called Rosie, told from the viewpoint of Don - Autie like Thomas and me

Thomas' dad doesn't speak to me look at me

Thomas doesn't care

'I have to go see these folks...' 'Can I come too?'

He's got his dad's beer perched awkward behind his orange juice while his dad is off powdering his nose

Dad returns and they vanish among the polite crowd

Books get signed

Networking happens

A speaking engagement for me at the University of Canberra - I love a uni gig

Students - young, full of fierce opinions and hope

Like Thomas

I smile at his easy youth

His ownership of that label which caused me so much pain at his age 'Asperger's'

"Ass burgers…'

God how I hated that little German surname.

I love the young ones

Creating our shared future

I can only tag on

Offering pointless advice

And tired, fat, middle-aged epithets.
But I don't mind

I'm happy for our world to lie in the hands of the young and their wisdom.

Being me

I am not the average

If indeed there is an average human.

I am a little quirky Purky person

'Out of left field'

They probably broke the mould, the kiln and the studio when I was made

I have more in common with the cat than his owner.

I am an anomaly

I am the convenor and sole member of the club for ex-prisoner, ex-homeless, home-owning, Masters graduate public servants

Committee meetings happen so often

Their minutes spell out my days and years.

I have motivation to power a small city

Determination to move the ocean

Love and joy to right the world.

I have this most confusing, broken, perfect life.

I cry one day and conquer mountains the next

I have endless time for humanity but spend my weekends alone, happily.
I shouldn't be - death should have come for me on countless days in my near-forgotten past

But who should be?

My life is incongruous and unlikely

As are the lives of all around me. Humanity is infinitely beautiful
Complex

Surprising.

I share the privilege of life with seven billion others

And it is good

Jeanette with velvet hippie hat, Whimsy Manor, 2017

When the brain is a pain: little bit creative, little bit crazy

I was diagnosed as Autistic in 1994. A year later I was diagnosed with schizophrenia. Apparently the mid-1990s was the time for these sorts of things. I have seen every kind of mental health professional, been in psychiatric hospitals in three states and many, many times. I take the sort of medication which changes you - what your body shape looks like, your energy levels but thankfully also - when it is working well - the way your brain functions to enable you to live a fulfilled life. Hopefully.

Mental health clinical settings are second nature to me but I hate them. I am an empath. I pick up on emotions of others intuitively. I can feel an angry person approaching before I even see them. Picture all that in a hospital ward where people are angry, sad, confused and suffering emotionally. Over 22 years I have built my self awareness, insight and level of control and agency. I struggle with my mental illness and all that comes with it but I usually come out of it OK. The poems in this chapter reflect on my experiences as a human being with a mental illness. There are some dark things here but also some humorous things and I hope some beautiful things too. A mental illness is not a thing to be ashamed of. I do not hide mine and if people have an issue with it, well I will know much sooner if I tell them. My illness is part of me too. I don't like her much but we are working on our relationship.

Untitled.   **[CW - alludes to sexual violence]**

Allen Ginsberg saw the best minds of his generation destroyed by madness...
Yet I am not of his generation

And I am not destroyed

Just a bit limited

Diminished
Judged.

'You were in the psych ward?' asks the suburban stereotype - she can't find words

What should she say to this alien refrain

'What was it like?'

Like it always is

The temple of disempowerment and infantilism

Of not listening to the mad people regardless of whether they say truth or delusion   Of useless bland medicated days worshiping the evil idol of daytime TV

Of allegiances formed and lost in hours and minutes

Of that strange equality where senior bureaucrat and drug addled homeless person sit at the same table

And converse in fractured knowing whispers

Of suspicious staff

Of uncomfortable, anxious visitors

Of activities which haven't changed since 1942

'Art' consisting of primary school projects and bright paint to offset dull moods

Ten pin bowling for those allowed to leave (22 years of illness has fostered in me an almost unnatural hatred of ten pin bowling)

Even basket weaving on occasion and with no acknowledgement of the irony.

The mad so often the sensitive folk who sad life has broken

The wildly intelligent, trapped in a world which treats them as children.

The assumptions

the prejudice

the mistrust for those supposedly helping

Jaded fifty-something nurses who have seen it all

Some are the caring

Some the uncaring

The lottery of which your case manager will be

'Damn, I got Tina'

The ensuing misery as you are ignored and invalidated your whole stay.

The not-so undercurrent of misery and violence

Men and women together

Immune to creepiness by dint of your illness

It happens at midnight when the nurses aren't watching
Weeks later you see the perpetrator and realise he is such
You thought he was your soulmate

Out of the fog of psychosis you see the reality

Blame yourself while trying to fend off his sickening advances.

The system

The structure

The evidently pointless rules.

You leave the universe of the psych ward behind and go back to your life as a public servant

or a big issue seller

This place is a great leveller.

You almost miss the predictable world of the hospital
The insular world

Where each person has a role and guaranteed audience
You go home to your empty house and hope to stay there
But you are never sure what the future holds.

Diagnosis - reflections on application of 'schizophrenic' to my me

You are a word

on a page

On every page written by doctors.

I hate you as I hate myself
I see you as I see myself
Defeated

Broken

Institutionalised.
My usual diagnosis

My old best enemy.

If I accept you then I need to accept Myself.

And that is insurmountably, impossibly, devilishly hard. Unwanted and unknown.

I skirt around the edges of you and the borders of my own self.
I deny you constantly, fervently.

A fight to the death where only one will win.

I see you as a friend of the medical profession
An excuse

A comma hanging unpronounced in the sentence of my life.

Yet even as I hate you and abhor you, I open the door a crack and let you sneak in.

I don't want you.

We fall together: Entwined: Embracing

with tensed forearms and gritted teeth.
I see the ground rushing toward me
Do we die together you and I

tangled together diagnosis and victim?
Or do I accept you and let your power dissipate leaving me

unharmed, calm, whole?

Lament of the deranged deity

I have a good problem
Too energised

Too happy
Too 'me'

Too many colours exploding everywhere like fireworks as I speak.
Sleep is unnecessary after three am

I leap up and wonder why every one is still asleep

There's work to do

I cuddle the cat

Have whole conversations with him in human and meow
I leave for work at 7 am

Get there and the lights turn on as I enter the space

Like I'm some kind of office deity

Cool

I'm productive

Do everything there is to do and look for more

'You're in a good mood!' says my boss

But it isn't good

The bus trip home gives rise to furious anger at the silliest things

Of course I'm confused

I think it's because I need the toilet

I yell at my long-suffering kitty

He hops on top of the fridge and licks his paws - he's been through this before

I make an appointment to see my psychiatrist - I figure that maybe I should I forget his name

Is it Tony?

Think Jeanette. I dredge through my mind to find the names of doctors Tony Attwood?

Tony Abbott?

It's not Tony but I don't know what it is

"Can I make an appointment to see the doctor?" (Problem solved)
When I get there he reassures me

'Your self-awareness will keep you safe'

'You are unique and skilled'

I am truly an impossible occurrence

I go home, comforted but still jangly and excitable

I feed the patient cat and watch TV

Reflect on this little skirmish in the intractable war between brain and me
You won't have me, illness

I know I'll never win but neither shall you

Another day, another battle, another tiny victory

And so it was and shall be for always

Not the best life, not the worst life

Just this life

My private universe

Sometimes I find myself in my private universe.

It is not utopia

or a pleasant daydream

It's Hell

if Hell were in this world.

My private universe is inhabited by ghosts

demons

death.
Satan and God are locked in there forever

In a war for my soul.

A red, spiky-haired imp that is my illness torments me
Tells me I am worthless

A loser

Evil

That life would be better if I weren't in it.

She designs my downfall hourly.

Jumps and cackles and dances

In a parody of happiness and joy.

I scream at her to leave me alone

But it just makes her laugh ever more loudly.

Everything is too meaningful - loaded, dripping with intent - in my private universe.

Objects take on wicked personalities

Auras appear around people

Strangers wander past my eyes and insult me
Colleagues bitch about me in furtive whispers
Insects work for ASIO

As do all my friends.

The only way out of here is to be with people who aren't subsumed
A strained smile here

And demented wave there.

A fractured attempt at a conversation.

My private universe is always lurking
Just out of reach

Lying next to reality

Within reality

Threatening to overwhelm me.

Medication supposedly springs me from its cell.
I look at the pills each night

Wondering how something quite that small

can do something quite so big.

It doesn't make a lot of sense.

My life's work is to banish my private universe or maybe to reconcile myself to its presence

so its power dissolves

and its influence diminishes and fades away.
I never know when I will find myself there again.

I thank Heaven for the days I am not there

And pray terrified prayers when I am engulfed by it.

Lost

[CW: suicide. This is not a poem for the faint hearted. If you aren't in a good place psychologically I would wait until you are before reading it. It bothers me and I wrote it!]

I thought of her as inconsequential. A quiet waif

wandering the halls

A sad smile on her face

which doesn't match her eyes.

She plays cards every night

In the kitchen.

One day she offers me a square of white chocolate. I say thank you.

We interact briefly

Discussing - or mentioning at least - the food the weather

the nurses.

She comes out on a sunny day an odd look in her eyes

'A nice day today' she says sadly
pointlessly.

A while later I wander in

slightly mad but improving

I see her boyfriend

(her husband actually. I discover this later in a moment of despair) His face looks ravaged

Destroyed

Eyes terrified

Pleading.

I briefly wonder if he has traded places with her to become a patient.
She's hung out to dry by her own hand.

I am broken

Ended.
There's no more doctors and nurses and patients anymore. Only people.

The next few days I spend urgently praying in the chapel
Concerned

No. That's not the word. There's no word for what I feel. The nuns think I'm a good woman for caring.
But I'm not caring to please them I don't care what anyone thinks
I'm in a private, suffocating world of regret.

When I leave the hospital I vow not to return. There's too much evil

Too much sadness there in her room

Room five.
She's alive at least.
I daren't ask of her. Not my place to ask

I imagine she's OK.

It's the only way I can assimilate what has happened.

She's OK I say over and over, willing myself to believe what I know to be unconvincing.

Simon, her husband will be caring for her I think

(I curse my doctor for telling me his name. It makes him closer, more of a friend, more invested in my world)

She will recover and see life for what it is - a beautiful, undeserved gift.

Months later I find out that this scenario did not happen.

She's gone to where Doctor Fitzgerald can no longer prescribe antidepressants or nurses check her obs and take her into the little office to talk through the day's events.

I am angry - not with her but with myself.

I should have known

Should have seen through the sad eyes into the hell that was her mind.
I didn't. Nobody did.
She is lost.

I give thanks for my life

Altered

Working working working working working I know to stop

Yet I can't stop

Onwards Onwards Onwards

I go to bed

Too late

The work flares in my head - a tsunami of necessity and function. So much to do

I see the wall

Little skulls

Thousands upon thousands upon thousands

Everywhere

New wall paper?

They change to swastikas

Hitler in my house?

How did he get in?

I don't want evil in here yet it's everywhere

 'My kitty I love you

Mr Kitty I love you

Mr Kitty I love you

Mr Kitty I love you

Mr Kitty I love you

.... Mr Kitty?'

I don't sleep

Or maybe I do

Is that killer fluff in the bathroom? Is this real?

What is real?

I get up and go to work

Why?

I tell my manager

Her concern seems weird

Out of proportionI feel OK

I'm just a little

altered.

I don't know here it will lead

It is fitting after the battle

I stand alone Strong Independent Real.

I am a product of the past. A beacon to my future.

Hardship lies around me

Strewn and scattered

All its power gone, pointless and spent.

I know my enemy

And manage to accept it Sometimes

Albeit infrequently.

The future glints out at me from the clouds

The fabled silver lining

A glimmering prize.

Something to strive for (if not a rainbow).

I aim to be comfortable in this now
This moment

Flawed as it is.

You will not destroy me world

You will not obscure my path, Self.

I am not afraid of the things which filled me with horror any longer I have outgrown their dominion and come into a place of power

Where only I stand

Capable and in control.

Free.

Green drawing, Jeanette Purkis 2016

Life: filling your hours full of minutes and cuddling your kitty

The chapter title says it all really! I wanted to finish this little poetry fest with some more fun poems as well as some observational ones and some reflection on what it is to be a funny little author person who is glued to her laptop all day and half the night, only stopping to go to her paid job, cuddle Mr Kitty and occasionally sleep for a bit! Mr Kitty inspired some of the poems in this chapter - as one would expect from such a singular and literary kitty. These poems are to savour and enjoy, like a beautiful sunset or a really funny and slightly inappropriate but unknowing act from a pet or small child.

Enjoy and enjoy some more, good readers.

Mr Kitty and Jeanette, Whimsy Manor 2018

When I get old...

When I grow old I'll complain at length about the ways of the day to anyone left long enough to listen.

I'll wear stylish clothes

makeup

heels

perfume - something suitably musky
I'll eat at the best restaurants

Go to the theatre, the opera

And secretly smoke cigarettes

And only let my closest confidantes in on the secret.
I'll watch adaptations of Agatha Christie

and every program on the ABC on a Sunday night.

I'll tell my friends and family that I don't drink then sneak the occasional sly glass of wine only publicly partaking at Christmas

I'll reminisce about my long-gone youth

(not all the stories will be true).

I'll live in a crumbling mansion.

I'll not-so-silently judge the youth of the day

And I'll push into supermarket queues

Thinking I have lived long enough to garner such a privilege.
I'll be a legend

A survivor

A historical character.

Sometimes I think I can hardly wait

until I get old.

On my feline friends and confidantes

I am a cat lady

Unashamedly

My life shared with feline friends

Each different.

Why?

What is 'cat' and why am I more aligned with people who have four legs and a purr?

I met cat for the first time at age three

Pined for a kitten every day until a little grey fluffy friend appeared when I was nine

Close to my very first adult act when moving out of home at 17 was to bring regal Sensei home

Sensei of the long fur and in-built compass sending her home whenever I moved

Sensei who followed me to work - a little loyal cat colleague

Sensei who left this world the day I also should have too

My grief for my little familiar unlike any grief before

Then Tilly the tiny tabby

Attitude beyond her small size

Visiting my public housing neighbours every day by knocking on the door with her naughty paw and waiting for them to invite her in

And they always did

And my current cat - although I never owned him. He is more friend than possession

Mr Kitty, the Autistic community's most famous cat with his own Facebook page and fans

His black feline self considered my housemate rather than my pet by pretty much everyone

He sits next to me as I work and bites my toes if I'm tardy with the cat food

I rescued him five years ago

And he rescues me every day

I hold him for endless moments and feel his purr

Bury my face in his softness when I'm overwhelmed and broken

Yes I am a cat lady with or without the 'crazy' epithet

Unashamedly

The Rearguard Vanguard

Monday morning she arrives at the office

The freezing air hurts her lungs

The usual union suspects in the foyer

Handing out their sad photocopied leaflets - black, white and red all over
The sign says 'strike tomorrow.'

She pointedly ignores the delegate with his misplaced enthusiasm and tired leftist sentiments

But they were her sentiments once

In some elusive past time

That other world

Of protests thick with youthful anger and we'll keep the red flag flying here...
Of meetings of thirty or so rag-tag students in smoky back rooms

The vanguard of the working class. Apparently

For her that dream died years ago

Despatched by the failings of the worker's party and their hypocrisy and disappointing humanity

Now she's faced with the passion - the obsession - of those who remained
The rear guard vanguard

The union delegate - hair red as fire, jeans and business shirt - tries to engage
"I vote Liberal" she lies easily

The delegate recoils just a bit and moves on to the next customer.

She marches through to the lifts

Heart racing a little and hands shaky

Starts the day

Aware of her twenty year-old self glaring down the years, eyes full of judgement.

The world turns once and the strike goes on without her
The rebels fail miserably to storm the winter palace
Nothing changes.
Nothing is new

She goes on with her work.

And Melbourne sparkles

A trip to Melbourne

My former home.

Conferences and book sales give way to tourism.

At the Victoria markets

I spy stalls amidst the fishy funk

A shop with felted hats and a hippie lady

We start to talk

If I took up her time I should buy something I think

I find a deep red yak wool scarf - it will be warm in Canberra's winter chill and wind

I bid her farewell, clutching a little plastic bag overflowing with my new scarf.

I head down the hill

There's a jewellery shop

Sparkly bling and a quiet girl hunched at the register, reading a book.

I search about, disappointed by the selection of things but wanting to buy
And then as I'm leaving a sparkly bracelet catches my eager eye

'How much?' I ask

The quiet girl's delicate features light up

'Ten dollars' she says.

Ten dollars for an endless amount of sparkles seems a very good deal.

I happily go back to my hotel

past a lanky young boy dancing to his headphones

A twenty-something lass with maroon ringlets

A family from the country, bumping into the unfamiliar crowds.

I have warm things, sparkles and joy.
My love for Melbourne is unabated.

Little panther

I have a little panther. He shares my home
With sleek black fur, golden eyes and ready purrs

I feel a thump each night as he leaps on the bed I see him coming towards me

Purposeful

On a mission for a cuddle

He flops down next to me and I hold his little paw

He talks

And talks

Announces his presence at times in plaintive meows or deep reverberating purrs

He asks for cuddles

Taps me on the shoulder as I work

'I'm here human person'

If I keep on at my work the tap gets more insistent until I scoop him up and bury my face in his soft fur

He steals my spot on the couch
'helps' with laundry

and gift wrapping

and cooking.

When I make the bed he insists on assisting

In his previous life he was a stray

He's like a rich boy fallen on hard times

When I cuddle him he cuddles back
An urgency of love

I was his saviour

And he was mine.

His entry to my world spelled the exit of my blighted existence

Since he has shared my hearth there have been no stays in modern day bedlam
No self-destructive dance of defeat

And when my fractured mind turns him into a demon

He walks up with his patented panther stride

And reminds me who he is

My mind's demon became reality's cat
I hold him and he purrs

Yes, I have a little panther who shares my home. I can scarce imagine life without him

The nation of me

If I were a country my national anthem would be written by Tracey Chapman

The coat of arms would be two crossed pens over a bookcase with a cat sitting on it

The floral emblem would be the rainbow rose

Citizens of the nation of me would be hardworking and kind and a little bit quirky
The national motto would be 'mum, it followed me home. Can we keep it?'

The main industry would be making art and exporting kind thoughts to places which need them

The currency would be poems

The national animal would be the cat...of course!

People would want to visit and stay and they would be welcome to

The county which was me would be preposterous

unviable

impossible

But it would somehow manage to thrive and be respected by other nations, despite - or because of - its quirks

Goodbye good readers.

Some parting thoughts - as I'm an author so I get to have them…Love your 'you', approach life as if it were a glass of delicious wine that you will only get one chance to enjoy. Listen to your favourite obscure and daggy music turned up loud and dance in the kitchen in your pyjamas. Remember that cats are discerning and those they select must have a good heart and also that nobody does enthusiasm like a dog!

I hope you have enjoyed visiting my inner world. Over the years I have made quite a career of oversharing. It works for me.

Mr Kitty has a few parting thoughts too:

.... "mraow! mraaaaaaow!! Meow!" (which translated is 'Please stop anthropomorphising me and give me some cat food and then cuddles human servant. And stop talking about dogs too!')

So goodbye from us both,Jeanette and Mr Kitty

Mr Kitty 2018

www.ingramcontent.com/pod-product-compliance
Lightning Source LLC
Chambersburg PA
CBHW042026150426
43198CB00002B/75